Are you sitting comfortably? Then I'll begin!

Exploring the role of storytime and its impact on young children.

hs

Are you sitting comfortably? Then I'll begin!

Published by

Corner To Learn Limited

Willow Cottage • 26 Purton Stoke

Swindon • Wiltshire SN5 4JF • UK

www.cornertolearn.co.uk

ISBN-10: 1-905434-10-3

ISBN-13: 978-1-905434-10-7

Text © Neil Griffiths 2006

Photographs of Neil in action! © Lis McDermott 2006

First published in the UK 2006

Edited by Helen O'Neill

Design by David Rose

Photography by Lis McDermott

Printed by Gutenberg Press Limited, Malta

Introduction

Storytelling and reading in this country are no longer the feature of daily life they once were. The introduction of computers, the compulsory television in a child's bedroom with DVD facility and, of course, pressure on valuable time have eroded once precious moments together 'telling tales'.

A glance back into our own history shows that story telling and story reading were a treasured part of family and community life. Stories were often passed on from one generation to another and regular re-telling created unique family memories.

The tradition of storytelling is still alive and well in many other countries and cultures, particularly those where books and written material are not easily available. Such cultures have the most wonderful collection of oral stories to be shared and passed on. To a large extent, we have lost this tradition in this country. Whilst some may still hold on to the dream that life is like *The Waltons* television series with Grandpa's nightly story to the family, reality paints a different picture. Fewer and fewer children are being told or read stories and, despite the easy access to a range of wonderful reading material, many homes still have a sparse collection of books.

Are you sitting comfortably? Then I'll begin.

3

> **"*I'm going to stop doing storytime. I just can't fit it in every day.*"**

Bookstart, which is a wonderful initiative, has ensured that many children begin their lives with a small collection of quality baby books, but there is much work to be done to encourage the importance of storytime and book-sharing at home. All is not well either in our pre-school and school settings. "I'm going to stop doing storytime. I just can't fit it in every day," was a casual comment in the staffroom of the school of which I was headteacher. It led me to the Storysack concept and my own passionate ten-year campaign to encourage storytelling.

In far too many settings, storytime is still a limited activity that conveniently fills a fifteen-minute gap before lunch or home time. 'Time' is, of course, regularly given as a reason. It is, however, an excuse, as time can and must be found both at home and school. Story-sharing is a key activity and a crucial component of a child's development into a mature reader. We must place as much emphasis on the development of a child's personal attitudes towards reading as we do on the technical skills that reading requires.

It must be our aim to encourage children to read because they **want** to, not because they **have** to, thus creating the beginning of a life-long love of books.

A chance to dream – the excitement of reading

The excitement of learning to drive is not the weekly lesson, practising the skills of three-point turns, parallel parking and hill starts, or acquiring the knowledge of the highway code. The excitement is the achievement and freedom of driving alone for the first time in your own car on the open road with the window down, your arm resting on the door, the stereo on full volume, sunglasses in position and the wind in your hair. A chance to dream!

Similarly, the excitement of learning to read is not the daily task of practising the skills of visual decoding, aural discrimination, phonetic awareness, word recognition, context clueing or acquiring the knowledge of the alphabet and English grammar. The excitement of reading is the achievement and freedom to choose your own reading material, discover a world of information and

Are you sitting comfortably? Then I'll begin!

5

adventure and be transported into real and imaginary worlds, visiting on the way the past, present and future. A chance to dream!

We must shift our emphasis and redress the balance. There has recently been an obsession with acquiring the skills and knowledge required for reading, which are of course highly important. However, we must now acquire a similar obsession for developing children's attitudes towards books and reading and to raising motivation levels.

Why tell stories?

For the purpose of this book, I am going to concentrate on reading rather than telling stories. Whilst both are equally important, most busy practitioners do not have the time available to memorize stories. Therefore the most common experience of early years settings is hearing a story being read.

Many would say that reading a story is a less complete form of communication than telling a story. The story reader is more conscious of the printed text and is offered less time

"Many would say that reading a story is a less complete form of communication than telling a story."

Are you sitting comfortably? Then I'll begin!

to actively engage with the audience. However, the skilled reader can still give a rich and memorable performance.

Since the beginning of mankind, stories have been important, above all for the pleasure and fun of the experience, both for the teller and the listener. For early years children, they are an opportunity to:

- enjoy a social experience with peers.
- listen carefully.
- contribute orally.
- become involved in role play and mime.
- extend memory and the ability to recall a story line.
- sequence a series of events.
- answer questions and share knowledge.
- understand the nature of a story, exploring plot, character, event, cause, conclusion, etc.
- be exposed to the work of many authors.
- hear great stories.
- enjoy the skills of a good storyteller.
- be exposed to rich vocabulary, phrasing, rhythm and rhyme.
- make sense of their own world.
- be transported into other imaginary or unvisited worlds and cultures.
- gain an insight into their own lives and the lives of others.

- experience the full range of human emotions.
- step out of the present into the future and past.
- create pictures in their minds.
- dream.

The list could go on!

Choosing stories: What makes a good story?

How many of us are guilty of quickly grabbing a book from the book corner for storytime and deeply regretting our choice minutes later? There is a great deal of poor material on the market and delightful illustrations and a lively cover can easily fool us. The search for a good story should never be compromised and time taken selecting material to read will pay great dividends later. So what makes a good story to read to young children?

Firstly, not all stories were written to be read aloud. Many books on the market today have been produced for a more personal experience. 'Flap' and 'turn' books, 'smell' and 'feel' books are not easy to use effectively in larger groups. Stories that use speech bubbles are also notoriously difficult to navigate, as are those that use highly unusual font size, shape and page positioning. A good test is to read the story aloud first. The reader can quickly assess its 'read aloud' qualities.

Children deserve to hear quality material and good stories for the young should have the following:

- an inviting cover

- simple, clear, bright, vivid illustrations

- attractive characters, believable or otherwise, that are few and well developed

- an interesting beginning that moves straight into the main plot

- a simple story line

- plenty of action

- suspense or events that surprise

- humour

- limited detailed background or lengthy description

- simple dialogue

- repeated phrases

- a great ending that both satisfies and surprises

"*Children deserve to hear quality material.*"

Good stories can also come in different shapes, sizes and formats. Practitioners should ensure that children are exposed to a wide range of material.

- story books
- board books
- big books
- cloth books
- bath books
- photographic books
- wordless books
  (These really challenge the story teller!)

Some settings successfully choose weekly themes for storytime, e.g:

- a collection of books by the same author
- a themed collection, e.g. weather, food, shopping, animals
- stories from other lands or cultures

Use should also be made of the rich selection of stories available from other cultures. *Letter Box Library* and *Mantra Publishers* have an excellent range.

12

Are you sitting comfortably? Then I'll begin.

When and where should stories be told?

I have often been pressured into telling stories in the most inappropriate settings, the worst being a shopping centre in Plymouth with 150 children under an escalator! Storytime essentially needs to be relaxed, unhurried and undisturbed.

For it to be a successful experience for all, a time should be chosen when the children are at their most alert and the storyteller high on energy levels. Why then do we choose to read stories fifteen minutes before lunch or at the end of the school day? Premium time for storytime is mid-morning and mid-afternoon.

> **"***Storytime essentially needs to be relaxed, unhurried and undisturbed.***"**

Flapjacks® storytime seating in action!

This book begins with the familiar old question, 'Are you sitting comfortably?' The answer almost always should be a resounding 'no!' (Have you sat on a hard floor for 20 minutes recently?) Comfort during a story is highly important. Cushions or small seats can help and, as we all have individual 'comfort levels', let some children lie down or curl up if they are comfortable. What is essential is that all children can easily hear and see you and you can also see all of them. Excellent storytime seats are available from *Corner To Learn* (www.cornertolearn.co.uk).

Storytime does not always have to be in a traditional setting, with children surrounding the teller who is in a comfy chair. Many schools and pre-schools have taken the time and energy to create special outdoor story areas in gardens, under willow arches, or beneath the branches of trees. Some have space, or have made it, to construct storytelling castles, boats, cottages or caves in previously poorly used areas of a building. Somewhere 'special' for storytime may seem a luxury, but many of us believe it is a basic requirement.

Imagine the excitement of the story *Hansel and Gretel* told deep in the heart of a wood or *Wind in the Willows* told by a riverbank. Storytime deserves to be elevated to such a special occasion.

Storytime should also find its way into all areas of the curriculum. What better way to introduce 'time' than

through the story *The Time it took Tom* (N. Sharratt and
S. Tucker)? A perfect companion to a lesson on
healthy eating is *The Very Hungry Caterpillar* (E. Carle),
and *Handa's Surprise* (E. Browne) is a wonderful vehicle
for the study of fruit. A perfect book for mathematical
exploration is *Walter's Windy Washing Line* by
Neil Griffiths.

Walter's Windy
Washing Line

by Neil Griffiths

Illustrated by Judith Blake

What makes a good storyteller?

"Storytime can be subdivided into five clear stages: preparation, introduction, delivery, interaction and review."

Firstly, the potential to tell stories well is in **all** of us. Some have a natural ability, in my case acquired from a magical storytelling father. Others can be taught the techniques and strategies for telling stories well. A prerequisite, however, is that all effective storytellers must be passionate about stories themselves and believe in the importance and value of exposing children to them. To be a storyteller and work with children requires the word 'actor' in their job description.

Storytime can be subdivided into five clear stages:

- **Preparation**
- **Introduction**
- **Delivery**
- **Interaction**
- **Review**

Preparation

- Read through the story once internally and once aloud.

- Plan possible questions to ask.

- Identify key moments in the story to emphasize or focus on.

- Plan the children's involvement.

- Review illustrations.

- Explore characters.

- Familiarize yourself with the plot.

- Look for opportunities to build up suspense and anticipation or add surprise.

- Plan your involvement as the reader, e.g. gestures, movements, voice.

Introduction

I remember my own storytimes at home, which were made magical by the innovative ways my father began a story. Sometimes he would give clues and often he would wear the clue! How could I ever forget the colander he wore as a space helmet for *Tin Tin goes to Mars*?

The moment a story begins is vitally important, as it can create the mood for the whole session. The reader should be demonstrating through their own body language that they are as excited as the audience.

A book can be introduced through:

- hints

- clues such as props and artefacts

- questions

- asking the children about their own experiences or knowledge of the subject matter

- sensory experiences (You have to eat fruit before *Handa's Surprise*.)

Shiver me timbers, lad!

- setting the scene
- raising expectation by rushing into the room as excited as can be
- sharing your own love of the story: "I just love this book and I know you will too!"
- hiding the book until the last moment

A regal introduction!

Once the book has been revealed, always leave a little time to look at the cover and talk about the title and author, but don't take too long as most children can't wait to get started.

'Pants' to this story!

Delivery

"It's not so much what is said, it's how it's said," my drama teacher once told me. However, he was naturally gifted and could make a gas bill sound interesting! But to an extent he was right. A great story can be destroyed by poor delivery.

> **"***Voice, gesture, facial expression and movement are the story reader's tools.***"**

It concerns me that so few practitioners have the opportunity during their initial training to be taught the strategies of 'engagement'. How often these days I hear a wonderful story read with the enthusiasm and energy of a solicitor outlining a will! As previously mentioned, we can **all** read stories and read them well. It just takes practice.

Firstly, it is important not to read a story for too long. Young children have a limited attention span. Fifteen minutes for 3- to 4-year olds and twenty minutes for 5- to 6-year olds is long enough.

Secondly, the story reader must be seen to be 'there' in the story itself and as absorbed as the audience are in the world the writer has created. Eric Maddern once wrote: "The voice is the storyteller's primary instrument – the words are the notes. Gesture and movement follow as secondary instruments." Voice, gesture, facial expression and movement are the story reader's tools.

Voice

The voice of the reader will add to the richness of the experience.

- Always avoid reading at the same level.

- Change volume, pace, tone and pitch.

- Build suspense by reading slowly.

- Build excitement by reading quickly.

- Don't worry if you can't achieve different accents. Simply change the depth or volume of your voice.

- Avoid a rhythmic or 'sing-song' style delivery. It is soporific.

- Practise clear diction.

- Play with your voice beforehand.

- Enlarge the voice as if in a theatrical performance.

Gesture

I like to feel that you can use your body like a giant paintbrush or sparkler to create images in the air with hands and feet when reading a story. If the book is held in one hand, there are still opportunities to bring the story to life with the remaining limbs!

> *Use arms and hands to draw imaginary pictures or to mime elements of the story.*

- Express moods, e.g. lower shoulders for sadness, show anger with clenched fists, shake the body to show fear.

- Turn pages at different speeds to create different moods.

- Peep over pages to create suspense.

- Use arms and hands to draw imaginary pictures or to mime elements of the story.

- Use the book itself to create shapes and images, e.g. wave the book like a bird in flight, point the book like a shark's fin, shake the book if the story has a 'chase' as part of the plot.

Are you sitting comfortable? Then I'll begin!

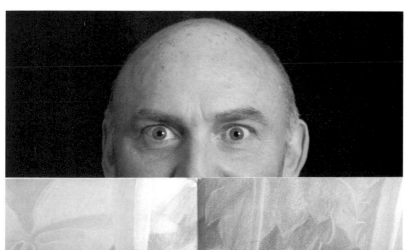

"_Use the book itself to create shapes and images._**"**

"_Peep over pages to create suspense._**"**

Are you sitting comfortably? Then I'll begin!

25

Facial expression

It is interesting to observe an audience of young children listening to a story. If watched closely, it can be seen that they fix their attention on the reader's face as much as on the illustrations themselves. They feed on the reader's expressed energy, excitement and mood.

Reading a story must become a theatrical performance and there is no place for inhibition when interacting with children. The expressions on the face of the reader are an essential element of any successful storytime. The face should express:

- atmosphere
- character and characterization
- humour
- anticipation and suspense
- a sense of the reader's own enjoyment of the story

Are you sitting comfortably? Then I'll begin.

29

Movement

Whilst there may be times when it is appropriate to snuggle up cosily on a soft seat to read a story, it is far too often an excuse to collapse at the end of the day. Movement from the reader can add drama and build images for children as the story unfolds. Too much movement can be distracting, but careful use can add greatly to a 'performance'.

The reader might:

- move slowly towards the children to build tension.
- move away to reflect faraway places in a story.
- rush across the floor, jump, slither or twirl to reflect movement suggested by a story line.
- stand, sit or lie down if it adds to the setting suggested in a story. For example, curl up when reading about Kipper in his basket (*Kipper's Toy Box*, M. Inkpen); stand on tiptoe when Sam hangs onto his kite (*Someone Bigger*, J. Emmett & A. Reynolds).
- move to different positions to read if a story suddenly changes scene or place.

"*Movement from the reader can add drama.***"**

Interaction

Many readers and tellers of stories prefer that a story never be interrupted. They believe that a break in a story destroys continuity and distracts from the

Are you sitting comfortably? Then I'll begin.

30

experience. With young children, I believe this to be unrealistic and undesirable. Focused participation should be welcomed as a central part of a storytime experience. However, the reader will need to take care not to lose the thread of the story and should ensure that the children's contributions relate to the story and not to 'last night's birthday party'!

During the story, the reader might:

- ask questions.

- encourage prediction.

- focus on illustrations.

- encourage sound effects.

- suggest role-play movements.

- focus on vocabulary.

- talk about character.

- encourage the children to join in with repeated phrases and favourite lines.

Readers can also have fun 'ad-libbing' or adapting a story line. A poor story often needs a 'lift' and adaptation can be quite desirable. Children who are following the story carefully will recognize changes and shout out with enthusiasm, 'It doesn't say that!' I regularly add twelve sausages, two chocolate bars and a bag of crisps to the list of food the Hungry Caterpillar ate!

It can be useful to ask another adult to watch you in action and provide feedback on how effectively you delivered the story. It is difficult to assess this yourself and these questions can be helpful:

❝A poor story often needs a lift.❞

- How do I look?

- How do I sound?

- Am I moving well?

- What signals am I giving you?

- What is it like for you?

- Did I involve you enough?

- Would you like to do it again?

Review

If a story has gone well, children will often burst into a spontaneous shout of 'Again, again!' This is encouraging to the reader and, if time allows, can be a wonderful opportunity to reinforce or enjoy a story again. However, a little time should always be found to reflect and review a story.

The reader might ask:

- Did you enjoy the story?
- Which was your favourite part of the story?
- How did you feel when …? (something happened)
- Did you like …? (character)
- Did you have a favourite picture?
- What kind of story was it? (humorous, action, etc.)
- Would you tell a friend to read it?
- Do you want to see the pictures again?
- Shall I read a favourite bit again?
- To assess the children's understanding, the practitioner might also ask a series of questions relating to the story.

Always ensure that these follow-up sessions are short and sharply focused as the impact of the story should not be lost.

"Time should always be found to reflect and review a story."

Reading stories – a summary

The following list can be a useful 'quick reference' before reading a story.

- Give it the time it deserves. Don't rush it. Make it a special time.

- Be in a positive mood.

- Tell children about the books you love.

- Read through the story first so you know the story line before reading it to your children.

- Build up the suspense before you begin.

- Collect props to add to the story, if available.

- Use positive body language.

- Use all of your body for meaningful gesture and movement.

- Use lots of facial expression.

- Use your voice well; think of volume, tone and speed.

- Build suspense through voice, face, body language, the way you turn the page.

- Change the pace to reflect tension.

- Hold the book in a positive way.

- Use the book to reflect the action in the story.

- Show enjoyment of illustrations.

- Ask questions.

- Predict what might happen next.

Are you sitting comfortably? Then I'll begin!

- Use sound effects.

- Enjoy doing actions together. Encourage your children to join in the role-play.

- Focus on interesting vocabulary.

- Ad-lib (make up bits for fun).

- Share your enjoyment.

Storytime in the home

While storytime in our school and pre-school settings is immensely valuable, its importance at home is even greater. Parents and carers are a child's first and most significant educators and no school reading programme can develop in isolation or without their support. Despite World Book Day and other national campaigns, fewer and fewer children are being read to in the home environment. Those who are being read to are not always being read to well.

Perhaps one of our greatest current challenges in education is to re-engage parents' support with reading at home and help them understand the critical role they must play if their children are to become successful, life-long readers. Many schools consider the obligatory book bag, which is for the most part grudgingly taken home, to be the most effective way parents can support their child's reading development.

I personally believe that for most parents and children this is an experience that they dislike and which is neither enjoyable nor effective in fostering a child's love of stories. Many schools send home structured scheme material. This encourages pressure, competition and over-emphasis on the skills of decoding and the material was never written for the purpose of a shared joy in stories.

Parents have two key roles to play at home if their children are to be given the best chance of becoming readers for life. They must **show** and **share**.

Show

Imitation can be a powerful force. One only has to watch local tennis courts fill during Wimbledon fortnight with 'would-be' Tim Henmans. Likewise, young children watch their parents intensely and young babies can often be seen holding a bath book as dad holds the newspaper. The reading habit can be infectious and parents must provide a positive role model, demonstrating their own enjoyment of reading by being seen doing just that.

Share

The sharing of stories must begin at home and the home environment can offer an intimacy rarely achievable in a school environment. The earlier it begins, the better. I greatly enjoyed reading to my new niece the moment she emerged from the labour theatre! Parents can share stories using all the skills and techniques suggested in this book, but many will need support.

"The sharing of stories must begin at home."

Are you sitting comfortably? Then I'll begin.

38

Pre-schools and schools could:

- home visit to introduce the importance of storytime.

- link with the public library service and jointly encourage membership.

- encourage parents to attend 'rhyme times' at libraries or offer them within school.

- offer training sessions on how to read and share stories.

- plan book week events involving parents.

- invite good story readers to demonstrate the skill to parents.

- encourage parents to benefit from the Bookstart scheme.

The single most important message to parents is, *Please find precious time to:*

- talk together.

- make reading a positive and enjoyable experience.

- enjoy rhymes.

- sing songs.

- be seen reading yourselves.

- visit bookshops.

- enrol your children in the local library.

The cultural diversity of this country brings its joy and challenges. For many children, English will not be their first language and storytime may well have to be adapted to help their understanding. Such children should not be prevented in any way from enjoying the full pleasure that hearing a story can bring. These children and their parents may also have a wealth of stories, oral or written, from their own culture, and practitioners should encourage them to share them regularly at home in their mother tongue.

Parents may also have the confidence to come into school and share these with a class. This should be welcomed and a translator could help those parents with limited English. Some of the finest stories ever written or told originate from other countries.

Above all, settings need to give a clear message to parents and carers that storytime and finding time to share a joint love of reading are essential if their child is to read for pleasure.

Key points

- Storytelling is no longer the feature of daily life that it once was.

- Reading stories to children is a key element of a successful reading programme.

- Children should read because they want to, not because they have to.

- The quality of stories chosen to be read should not be compromised.

- An appropriate time and environment should be found to hear stories regularly.

- Those who read stories must be passionate about them and believe in their importance.

- Reading a story should become a theatrical experience.

- There is no room for inhibition and we can all read stories well with practice and training.

- Parents and carers are children's first and most important readers of stories.

Are you sitting comfortably? Then I'll begin!

41

Conclusion

If we want to prevent a generation of children failing to discover the joy of reading, we must reverse the trend. The challenge is to convince parents, families and practitioners alike that storytime is a child's right, not a privilege, and one of the most precious gifts that they can give their children is to find time to share a story together.

Bibliography

Colwell, Eileen, *Storytelling*, Thimble Press, 1991

Maddern, Eric, *Storytelling at Historic Sites*,
    English Heritage, 1992

Read aloud with Neil Griffiths storybooks. Visit *redrobinbooks.com*

Did you see them too? (Red Robin Books)

Florence was no ordinary Fairy (Red Robin Books)

Grandma and Grandpa's Garden (Red Robin Books)

If Only (Red Robin Books)

Itchy Bear (Red Robin Books)

The Journey (Red Robin Books)

Messy Martin (Red Robin Books)

Mrs Rainbow (Red Robin Books)

No room for a baby roo! (Red Robin Books)

Ringo The Flamingo (Red Robin Books)

Who'd be a fly? (Red Robin Books)

Winnie Wagtail (Red Robin Books)

Walter's Windy Washing Line (Corner To Learn)

Anything's Possible (Storysack)

Grandma Brown's Three Fine Pigs (Storysack)

The Scarecrow Who Didn't Scare (Storysack)

Are you sitting comfortably? Then I'll begin!

Training

Neil Griffiths offers a series of highly acclaimed workshops on a number of topics:

- **Mathematics through story** – This highly practical workshop will explore the use of story and rhyme in the development of activities across the mathematics curriculum.

- **Let's Learn!** – A practical and informative in-service training, focusing on innovative and effective ways to engage and motivate children.

- **A Corner to Learn!** – This acclaimed workshop is a fantastic source of inspiration for making and using play corners. Designed for all early years settings including nurseries, playgroups and primary schools.

- **So you want to read a story?** – This workshop introduces Storysacks, an exciting literacy concept that has received national and international recognition.

- **Takes a moment ... lasts a life-time!** – A thought-provoking and highly practical course aimed at all practitioners working with young children from birth to seven. This training opportunity examines the complex process of planning an appropriate and inspiring curriculum for young children.

If you would like to book a workshop or receive further information, please contact:

Corner To Learn Limited
Willow Cottage • 26 Purton Stoke • Swindon
Wiltshire SN5 4JF • UK
Telephone / Fax: **+ 44 (0)1793 421168**
e-mail: **neil@cornertolearn.co.uk**
web: **www.cornertolearn.co.uk**